History and Prospects

OF THE

EVANGELICAL ALLIANCE,

1859.

LONDON:

OFFICE OF THE EVANGELICAL ALLIANCE,

7, ADAM-STREET, STRAND (W C.)

1859.

LONDON: PRINTED BY W. J. JOHNSON, 121, FLEET STREET.

HISTORY AND PROSPECTS
OF THE
EVANGELICAL ALLIANCE.

OFFICE OF THE EVANGELICAL ALLIANCE,
7, ADAM STREET, LONDON,
January 1859.

THE Committee of Council, urged by many considerations, feel it right, at the present period, to invite attention to the following succinct statement:—

It is intended, trusting to God for His blessing, to spread the Alliance through the United Kingdom. Wherever there is a body of brethren, one in faith and love, and anxious to be more so—desirous to be in connexion with the entire body of Christ in all lands—and wishing the Church to be in a state of readiness for coming events—there, God helping them, they will try to plant a Committee, and introduce Membership, of the Alliance.

Preparatory to this result, it is desirable that Christian people should know what the Alliance has done, and what it proposes to do. The following is a brief outline of the HISTORY AND PROSPECTS OF THE EVANGELICAL ALLIANCE.

In 1845, an invitation, signed by fifty-five Scottish Ministers and Laymen, convened a meeting at Liverpool, to consult on the best means of promoting Christian Union. Two hundred and sixteen Englishmen responded to the call. This was the origin of the Evangelical Alliance.

The members met last autumn in the same city, animated by the same spirit, but with clearer views as to the future founded on thirteen years' experience of the past.

During the interval, the Evangelical Alliance had taken root in various countries. France, Germany, Switzerland, Sweden, Turkey, India, are among the chief. Since the Evangelical Alliance was finally constituted, in 1846, three Assemblies of Christians of All Nations have been held in the three chief languages, and at the three principal capitals, of Europe;—in London, during the Exhibition of 1851 ; in Paris, during that of 1855 ; and in Berlin, under the sanction and patronage of the King of Prussia, in 1857.

Within the period named, the Evangelical Alliance has aimed at three main objects: The diffusion of a greater spirit of harmony among Christians of various communities at home ; the defence of Religious Liberty in foreign countries ; and the initiation of various enterprises for the direct work of the Gospel in Heathen, Mohammedan, and Christian countries.

I. *Harmony of Christians.*—This is the great and cardinal work of the Alliance. We desire Union for Union's sake. That end is, by itself, the most grand, the most practical thing that human heart can conceive. The object is obligatory upon us by the law of the Lord Jesus Christ, and it is the first duty of Christians to aim at it.

This was well expressed at the Constituent Conference of August, 1846 :—

"That, inasmuch as this proposal for Union originated, in a great degree, in the sense very generally entertained among Christians, of their grievous practical neglect of our Lord's 'new commandment' to His disciples, to 'love one another' (in which offence the members of the Alliance desire, with godly sorrow, to acknowledge their full participation), it ought to form one chief object of the Alliance to deepen in the minds of its own Members, and, through their influence, to extend among the disciples of the Lord Jesus Christ generally, that conviction of sin and short-coming in this respect, which the blessed Spirit of God seems to be awakening throughout His Church ; in order that, humbling themselves more and more before the Lord, they may be stirred up to make full confession of their guilt at all suitable times, and to implore, through the merits and intercession of their merciful Head and Saviour, forgiveness of their past offences, and Divine grace to lead them to the better cultivation of that brotherly affection which is enjoined upon all, who, loving the Lord Jesus Christ, are bound also to love one another, for the truth's sake which dwelleth in them.

"That the great object of the Evangelical Alliance shall be, to aid in manifesting, as far as practicable, the unity which exists among the true disciples of Christ; to promote their union by fraternal and devotional intercourse; to discourage all envyings, strifes, and divisions; to impress upon Christians a deeper sense of the great duty of obeying their Lord's command, to 'love one another,' and to seek the full accomplishment of His prayer, 'That they all may be one, as thou Father art in me, and I in thee; that they also may be one in us: that the world may believe that thou has sent me.'"

Now, of the changed aspect of the United Kingdom in this respect, it is needless to speak. No one who knows the facts can hesitate to admit that the alteration is very great. Among Evangelical persons, cordial feeling towards one another is now the rule, and the contrary the exception. It used to be the reverse. This improved state has not been gained by unworthy concessions. Men have not ceased to hold opposite views of Church and State, but they have learned to put those views in their proper place, and to regard them as secondary. We claim this result as greatly owing to the Evangelical Alliance. Its membership, consisting of only a few thousand persons, is by no means the measure of its influence. It has raised the question of Christian Union in the public mind. The conscience of pious Protestants, thus appealed to, has everywhere given but one verdict. The duty of moderation in controversy, of generous allowance for differences of judgment, and of cordial affection towards all the true disciples of Christ, are now very generally recognised.

At the same time there is much more to be desired than

has been hitherto attained; and the Committee still recognise it as their chief privilege and duty to direct the efforts of the Alliance to this end. They will not cease, in dependence upon Divine aid, to cultivate the spirit of brotherly love among Christians, and to call it forth in open manifestation before the world. With a view to this end they especially desire to promote meetings for united prayer, either periodical, or, where that cannot be attained, on special and urgent occasions, in the conviction that those who pray together will, by that very exercise, find themselves drawn into permanent union, and be best prepared to act together whenever the claims or the exigences of Christ's kingdom require it.

II. *Religious Liberty.*—The services to Religious Liberty have not been inconsiderable.

1. ITALY.—(1.) The liberation of Dr. Achilli from the Inquisition in 1849 was effected by the Evangelical Alliance. Questions subsequently raised about his conduct, do not alter the merits of the case. Dr. Achilli was imprisoned for being a Protestant, and it was our consequent duty to release him. The French and British Branches sent a deputation to Rome to ascertain facts; and a second deputation went from England to Paris to influence the Prince President. With all the aid of our Ambassador, the Marquis of Normanby, nothing was at first effected. At last, the Evangelical Alliance, through its friends in Scotland, arranged for deputations from the great Scotch cities, headed by the Provosts, to be ready to wait upon the President, Louis Napoleon, who, wisely yielding to the force of public opinion, sent orders by telegraph to Rome for Achilli to be allowed to escape.

(2.) The Madiai also under God owed their release to the Evangelical Alliance. An exclusively English movement for their liberation was proceeding slowly when the Geneva Committee of the Alliance sent a deputation to England to ask that the effort might be made European. The consequence was, the departure from each Protestant Capital of Europe of Christian delegates to Florence.

The united mission, by God's blessing, prevailed. The result was obtained, technically at the request of the French Government, but virtually by means of the Christian public opinion of Europe. It may be interesting to add, that Francisco and Rosa Madiai are at this time keeping a depository for Bibles and Testaments at Nice, and aiding considerably the dissemination of the Word of God through the North of Italy.

(3.) When the King of Sardinia was in England, an address, originated by the Evangelical Alliance, was presented to his Majesty, thanking him for the Religious Freedom established by the Statuto, and asking him to carry it out to the full extent. The answer, signed by the King in autograph, promising that this shall be done, is suspended in the Council-room of the Alliance.

2. GERMANY.—The efforts made to prevent the lesser Protestant States of Germany from interfering with the religious liberty claimed by Evangelical Dissenters have been, to a great extent, successful. The King of Prussia, appealed to by the Evangelical Alliance, threw the weight of his influence into the scale. His Majesty personally has always responded to applications made to him in regard to Prussia itself.

3. SWEDEN.—A similar appeal, originated by the Evangelical Alliance, was this summer laid before the Swedish Ambassador, and through him was communicated to the Government of Sweden, occasioned by the condemnation to exile and confiscation of six converts to Romanism. It is signed by the Archbishops of Canterbury and Dublin, and several of the Bishops; by Lord John Russell, and Members of Parliament of all parties; by numerous Peers, including three former Lord Chancellors; and by leading Ministers of all the British Churches. At the instance of the London Committee, acting chiefly through Foreign Committees of the Alliance, appeals to the same effect, addressed to Sweden, have since issued from Turkey, Hungary, Piedmont, Canton de Vaud, Geneva, Holland, and America. France had previously taken a similar step. The addresses from the extreme East and West bear

as remarkable signatures as the English. The Turkish includes eminent converts, many of them Ministers, from the Greeks, Armenians, and Turks; all the American Missionaries within reach; British, American, French, and German Merchants; Managers and Auditor of the Ottoman Bank, British Chaplains, Scotch and French Ministers of the Gospel, the State Physician to the Sultan, &c. The American includes a great body of Bishops, Judges, Members of Congress, Members of State Legislatures, with Clergymen and Laymen of all denominations.

4. TURKEY.—A memorial, addressed to the Sultan of Turkey, from the Christian Conference of Paris, in 1855, in behalf of Religious Liberty, was presented to his Majesty's Ministers by a deputation from the Constantinople Committee of the Evangelical Alliance. Simultaneously, memorials in favour of Christian Liberty in Turkey, were addressed to the principal Christian Sovereigns, and several satisfactory replies were received. It is not too much to say that these steps powerfully contributed to the concession of the celebrated Hatti Humaioun.

5. DENMARK, RUSSIA, &c.—Proceedings in regard to the use of the German language in the churches of Schleswig and Holstein (German Duchies of Denmark), and in regard to printing the Bible in the vernacular language of Russia, took place at the Berlin Conference of 1857, and various steps of the same sort have at different times been adopted.

III. *Enterprises Initiated.*—One chief use of the Evangelical Alliance has been to bring out public feeling and set it to work in relation to passing questions:—

1. TURKISH MISSIONS.—When war broke out in Turkey, an Association was fostered by the Evangelical Alliance, to direct British sympathy in an increased measure towards Missions in that Empire. The Turkish Missions-Aid Society has been the means of greatly extending among English Christians an acquaintance with the operations of the Board of American Missions. It has contributed

largely to the support of the native agency employed by that Board, and has been the chief cause of the new Mission to Bulgaria. It has also contributed to the work of the English Bishop at Jerusalem.

2. ANGLO-TURKISH LITERATURE.—Out of the Turkish Missions Society has grown the Association for Anglo-Turkish Literature. Aided by influential friends, it has caused Dictionaries, Grammars, and Vocabularies to be prepared for teaching English to the Turks—thus strengthening the hands of the Missionaries. Having laid an ample foundation for one language of the empire, it is now preparing to do the same for another—the Arabic. When this is done, the Committee will attempt other dialects of the same Empire. It is not too much to say, that but for the Evangelical Alliance, this Committee would not have existed.

3. GERMAN COMMITTEE.—On the return of the British members from the Berlin Assembly last year, it was determined to found a Committee for Correspondence with Germany, with a view to ultimate co-operation. The Committee, though distinct from the Evangelical Alliance, has been fostered by it. It has corresponded with leading Christian men of Germany, and is now publishing their letters. The Committee has received the cordial support of the Archbishop of Canterbury and of the Bishop of London. It is on the eve of proposing plans for rendering British aid to German evangelisation, and is in communication with numerous friends at home and abroad, in reference to plans for Continental Refuges for seceding Roman Priests.

4. INDIAN COMMITTEE.—At the First Annual Conference of the Evangelical Alliance after the outbreak in India, steps were taken to combine the Christian people of the United Kingdom, for promoting Christian Vernacular Education in the thirteen chief languages of that Peninsula. A practical suggestion to the same effect had been thrown out in a paper of the Church Missionary Society. The Evangelical Alliance resolved to lend its aid

to reduce that proposal to practice. A Special Committee was appointed by the Annual Conference on the subject. That Committee invited the Secretaries and leading Friends of the great Missionary Societies to a meeting at the office of the Evangelical Alliance. The outline of a plan was there read and approved, and a resolution passed commending it to the sympathy of Protestant Christians. Successive meetings were subsequently held at the Caledonian Hotel, and St. James's Hall, at which the scheme was matured and finally settled. The Committee for Indian Education is now in full operation.

5. FRENCH COMMITTEE.—After Orsini's late attempt to assassinate the Emperor of the French, meetings were held in the office of the Evangelical Alliance, and plans formed for exerting a religious influence over the multitudes of French Refugees in London. A Committee is formed, with good prospects of success, especially in the education of the young.

6. MISCELLANEOUS SCHEMES.—It would be tedious to state all the practical objects for which the Evangelical Alliance has exerted itself, by appointing Provisional Committees, and in other ways. The General Committee for the Protection of the Lord's-day, with especial reference to Sunday Bands and the Crystal Palace, was constituted by the joint action of the Evangelical Alliance and the Church of England Society for Promoting the Observance of the Lord's-day. A Spanish Committee has expended a considerable sum on printing the Scriptures in Madrid. An Italian Committee, under the presidency of the late Sir Edward Buxton, has been in some degree instrumental in reconciling denominational differences in Italy, and in promoting the spread of the Gospel.

7. THE CHRISTIAN PRESS.—Prizes of £100 each have been given for the best Essays on Popery, Infidelity, and the Sabbath—subjects in relation to which Evangelical Christians are, for all practical purposes, unanimous. The Essays of Dr. Wylie on the Papacy, of the Rev. Mr. Pearson on Infidelity, and of the Rev. Mr. Hill on the Sabbath, are

well-known, and deservedly appreciated throughout the Christian Church. Separate prizes on Infidelity, competed for by working men, also brought out the valuable essays of Mr. C. M. Smith (printer), and Mr. M. Spears (ironfounder), and others. The monthly organ of the Committee, *Evangelical Christendom*, is rendering good service to Christian Union and the Evangelisation of Europe. The *Bulletin du Monde Chretien*, the *Kirche des Herrn*, now succeeded by the *Neue Evangelische Kirchen Zeitung*—*New Evangelical Church Gazette*—(which is commended to the Christians of Germany by no less than sixty of the leading theologians and other eminent persons of its various States and Kingdoms), and the Swedish organ of the Alliance have followed its lead.

8. COMBINED PRAYER.—At the origin of the Evangelical Alliance, in 1846, Concerted Prayer for the Church, for the World, and for Christian Union, was recommended to be offered by Christians every Monday forenoon. The proposal was confirmed at the Paris Conference in 1855, and the request signed by two friends from each of the nations of France, England, Germany, Switzerland, Italy, Holland, Belgium, Denmark, Sweden, the United States, and Turkey, has been circulated in various languages in Europe and America. Every other practical step sinks into insignificance compared with this measure of the highest Christian utility as well as of duty.

9. PREACHING TO THE MILLION.—On December 9, 1855, Exeter Hall was opened by the Committee of the Evangelical Alliance for preaching sermons to the working people of London, to be delivered by Ministers of different denominations. Following up this beginning, on the 24th of May, 1857, a Committee of Members of the Church of England entered upon the work. Clergymen and dignitaries of the Established Church preached in succession, introducing the Litany into the worship. The effort was stopped, as is well known, by a proceeding in the Ecclesiastical Courts. Thereupon, Nonconformists took it up, adopting the Litany and hymns previously used. The

ecclesiastical obstacles having been removed, the clergy resumed the services. Simultaneously, St. James's Hall is occupied by Nonconformists. Soon after Exeter Hall was occupied by the clergy, Westminster Abbey was opened for evening services, and St. Paul's and other cathedrals and churches in different parts of the country have since followed. Services in secular buildings were commenced by the Evangelical Alliance, and it is a matter of devout thankfulness to all sincere Christians that they have been followed in cathedrals and churches and other places of Divine worship.

Such, in the general outline, is the retrospect of the Evangelical Alliance up to the recent Conference at Liverpool. Whatever good has been done, must be ascribed exclusively to that merciful Saviour who has condescended to make use of such imperfect agency. The Committee refer, therefore, to the past, not as if they had anything to boast of, but solely to give an idea to their friends of what the union of Christians is capable of doing, if rightly, wisely, and methodically applied. They think that the times require such an institution as the Alliance, and in this belief they call upon the friends of Christian union to rally round it.

The Chinese war having terminated, the Liverpool Conference appointed a Committee to confer with friends of Missions on the practicability of acting together for Chinese Christian education, as was done (in 1857) for Indian education. The same inquiry is to be made about Turkey.

The moral sense of the country having been offended by the use of the Confessional among a section of the English clergy, an united testimony was recorded against the practice.

Declarations of the Secretary of State for India about *neutrality* in religion having caused general anxiety, and Sir John Lawrence's views having as generally commended themselves, resolutions were passed in favour of a Christian policy, which were forwarded to Lord Stanley, and which will show statesmen that there is a substantial agreement among Churchmen and Dissenters on that subject.

The German schemes already mentioned were discussed, and the Gustavus-Adolphus Society commended, for the first time, by a formal resolution, to British Christians. The continued intolerance of Mecklenburg-Schwerin towards Dissenters having been represented, steps were again taken in relation to it. Systematic visitation from England of Protestants in the Roman Catholic provinces of Austria, and other Romish portions of Europe, was considered. Expressions of affection and sympathy were addressed to His Majesty the King of Prussia, and a communication was made to the Regent respecting the religious liberty promised last year to Dissenters by the King. These have been forwarded by the Ambassador.

The seizure of a Jewish child by the Pontifical authorities at Bologna, having called forth the indignation of all European countries, and even of the Austrian and French Governments, communications were addressed from the Conference to the Jews of England, expressive of hearty sympathy, to which a grateful response has been made by the Central Committee of the British Jews.

The proceedings of Protestant Europe in regard to Sweden were reported, and steps were resolved upon to influence the French Government to do for Protestants in France what Protestants, through Europe, have done for the Swedish co-religionists of the Emperor.

In following up these last resolutions, the Committee have been exceedingly anxious to see the exact path of duty in regard to the French Government; they are in communication with the Jewish body, and with the Protestants of Christendom, and they hope ere long to take energetic measures for resisting priestly persecution in France and Italy—measures on behalf of which they solicit, before hand, the prayers of all true Christians.

The effect of the Liverpool Conference on many earnest minds in that town has been highly gratifying. Sixteen of the clergy have signed a document, in which, after saying that "the Evangelical Alliance is an object deserving, to say the least, the prayerful examination of ministers of the Church of England," they add, "With this view, we desire a consultation among clergymen of the Church of England who sincerely wish for the union of the Christian people of the United Kingdom, Germany, Holland, France, the United States, and the other countries of the world and who only hesitate as to the best mode of effecting it; and we shall be glad if such a meeting can be held in London, to be attended by a Deputation to explain the position, prospects and principles of the Alliance."

This document is signed by the Rev. Dr. McNeile; the Rev. A. Knox, Perpetual Curate of Birkenhead; the Rev. J. B. Lowe, Incumbent of St. Jude's; the Rev. W. R. Hunt, Incumbent of St. Columba's; the Rev. L. H. Thomas, Incumbent of St. James's, Toxteth Park; the Rev. J. C. Powell, Incumbent of St. Thomas's, Toxteth Park; the Rev. H. Woodward, Incumbent of St. Clement's, Toxteth Park; the Rev. S. Payne, late Incumbent of Hunstanworth; the Rev. H. E. F. Vallencey, Vicar of Sutton, St. Helen's; the Rev. W. H. Wright, Incumbent of Christ Church, Everton; the Rev. R. D. Powell, Incumbent of New Brighton, &c., &c.

The Resolution of the Committee of Council on this subject may fitly close this Statement of Facts:—

Resolved—"That the Chairman do convey to Dr. M'Neile, and, through him, to the other clergymen who have signed this encouraging document, the expression of our Christian thankfulness for a proposal so indicative of their desire to promote the great object for which the Alliance was formed, and with a view to which its operations are carried on, both in this country and other parts of the world. We desire nothing more than that that institution should be rendered as efficient as its aims are Scriptural; and will endeavour to give as complete a view of its foreign, as well as domestic, usefulness, at a meeting to be held early in 1859, as it lies in our power to present; and we hope that the Evangelical clergy, generally, will take a serious and prayerful interest in the question then to be raised, and throw the weight of their influence into such measures, promotive of the union of all true and sincere Christians, as may appear to them to be required by the state of the world, the exigencies of the universal Church, and the honour of the Lord Jesus Christ."

Such being the past history and present position of the Alliance, its plans, as regards specific subjects, must greatly depend, from year to year, and month to month, upon Divine Providence. The times teem with religious events. As these happen, the Evangelical Alliance will facilitate their discussion, and try to ascertain the mind of the Church of God upon them. Where brethren are persecuted, they will ask for prayer and attempt relief. Where doors are opened to the Gospel, they will direct attention, and urge to united action.

At home the Committee will continue to throw any weight they can into Sabbath observance, and to counteract, as best they may, Popery and Infidelity. They will especially and above all, in proportion to the agency they possess, multiply centres of Christian peace through the kingdom—hoping that love, generosity, and piety, will radiate all around, from each new Committee of the Alliance so formed. What Missions are to the world, the Alliance will endeavour to be to the Church—preaching mutual peace among Christians, as Missionaries preach peace with God to the unconverted. According to the measure in which Christian people give funds, the Alliance will multiply agency, extend the use of the press, perfect their periodical, facilitate Christian intercourse by social meetings and other means, and indefinitely extend correspondence with foreign Christians.

The friends of Christ will see, in the foregoing History of the Alliance, palpable marks of God's blessing—in its prospects, as now stated, ample work to be done for God. It is scarcely necessary to add that, if this be true, a duty devolves on every true Christian to aid it by his prayers, influence, and money.

In conclusion, the Committee advert to their pecuniary position and prospects. From various causes, they have had to contend with great difficulties. The work they have done has involved a considerable outlay, while they have had an inadequate exchequer. The debt which was incurred as the consequence must be extinguished and a working capital be raised. In part this is already done by some of the old and ever generous friends of the Alliance, in the confident hope that others also will lend their aid. The Committee, while looking, on the one hand, to an augmented income, are aware, on the other, of the necessity of guarding against an expenditure beyond their means. More attention will be given by a Finance Committee to this object, without whose consent no expense is in future to be incurred. With this security and check provided, they are confident that they may appeal to their friends and reckon on their support. The proposal is to raise 1,000*l.* If this sum is realised, it will defray all existing liabilities, and leave a surplus of 150*l.* The contributions already received and promised amount to 500*l.* The members of the Alliance are more than sufficiently numerous to provide all that is required for the present annual expenses, did they all subscribe even a moderate sum. If exigent cases arise demanding extraordinary efforts, they will, no doubt, be met by a corresponding liberality.

The Committee of Council have only to add that the Rev. W. CARDALL, M.A., late Vicar of Budbrooke, Warwickshire, and Association Secretary of the Church Missionary Society; and the Rev. JAMES DAVIS, late Minister of the Independent Church in Rochester, have been appointed Official Secretaries.

Signed on behalf of the Committee of Council,

9 781535 805407